Here is Pip.

GW01237959

What is Mouse doing?

A thank you letter.

Dear Gran,

Thank you for the rocket.

From,

Mouse

What is Jojo doing?

A thank you letter.

Dear Gran,
Thank you for the doll.
With love from,
Jo

Pip wants to do
a letter too.

Pip's letter.

What is Mouse doing?

Licking and sticking.

Mrs V Macdonald
6 Crispen Road
Newtown
NT 17 0P8

What is Jojo doing?

Licking and sticking.

Mrs V Macdonald
6 Crispen Road
Newtown
NT17 0P8

Pip does licking and sticking too!

Pip gives Mouse his letter.

Jojo laughs.

"What does it say?" asks Jojo.

"It says DEAR GRAN, THANK YOU FOR THE CHOCOLATE. I LOVE IT!" says Mouse.

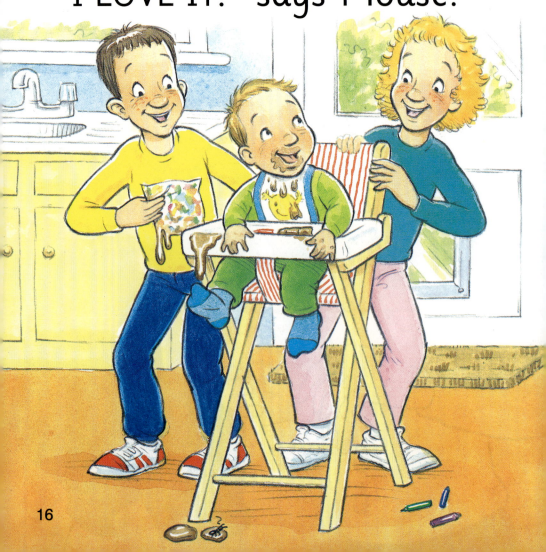